THE COMPLETE
WIT AND WISDOM
OF THE IRISH

THE COMPLETE WIT AND WISDOM OF THE IRISH

Des MacHale

Illustrated by Tony Blundell

ANGUS & ROBERTSON PUBLISHERS

ANGUS & ROBERTSON PUBLISHERS

16 Golden Square, London W1R 4BN,
United Kingdom.

First published in the United Kingdom
by Angus & Robertson (UK) in 1988
Reprinted 1988

Copyright © Des MacHale 1988
Illustrations © Angus & Robertson (UK) 1988

Typeset by New Faces, Bedford
Printed by Hazell Watson & Viney, Aylesbury

British Library Cataloguing in Publication Data.
MacHale, Des
    The complete wit and wisdom of the Irish
    I. Title.
    828.'91409   PN6178.I6
    ISBN 0 207 15859 2

CONTENTS

INTRODUCTION

The dictionary defines an Irish Bull (the best definition of Irish Wit and Wisdom there is) as 'an expression containing a contradiction in terms or implying a ludicrous inconsistency in speech frequently unperceived by the speaker'.

In other words, nothing more than the way they speak in Ireland, nothing more than the way their peculiar minds express themselves – their thoughts and words tripping over themselves in a relatively recent and alien tongue. To the unsubtle listener, these examples of Irish wit and wisdom may indeed sound like a contradiction when taken literally, but the philosopher will realise that at times these Irish Bulls contain a deep truth.

This book is indisputably the greatest ever collection of Irish wit ever assembled in one volume. Many of them are genuine, as anybody who's ever been to Ireland will know. And Pat and Bridget, together with their friend Mike, are prototype Irish-people who, as well as spawning a million Pat and Mike jokes, have also created an art form where the definition of the art form is itself an example of the art form: 'If there were twelve Irish cows lying down in a field and one of them was standing up, then that one would be an Irish Bull.'

— 1 —
DEATH

THE Irish are one of the few nations who are capable of dying laughing – in fact it might be claimed that they invented the concept of the jovial wake or the dead man's last party.

PAT and Mike were passing a cemetery.

'What's that, Pat?' asked Mike.

'That's a cemetery, Mike,' said Pat, 'that's where all the dead people live.'

PAT'S next-door neighbour had died and was lying in his coffin with a great big smile on his face.

'Why is he smiling?' Pat asked the man's widow.

'Well, it's like this,' said the widow, 'he died in his sleep and he doesn't know he's dead yet. He's dreaming he's still alive, and what I'm afraid of is that when he wakes up and finds out he's dead, the shock will kill him.'

PAT was talking with the local undertaker who told him that business had never been worse – he hadn't buried a living soul for over six months.

PAT was attending a neighbour's funeral, a man who when alive had not suffered fools gladly.

'Do you know what I'm going to tell you,' he said to Mike, 'if that man was alive today he would turn in his grave to see some of the people who came to his funeral.'

MIKE was delivering the graveside oration for an old friend of his who was being buried.

'That man in the coffin,' he thundered, 'is a living proof of the fact that hard work never killed anyone.'

'YOU can't escape fate,' Mike used to say, 'show me a place where people don't die and I'll go and end my days there.'

PAT and Mike were watching the wall being built around the new graveyard.

'Progress is a great thing and cannot be halted, Mike,' said Pat. 'That's the graveyard I hope to be buried in, if the good Lord spares me.'

'IS your father long dead?' Mike asked Pat.

'Well,' said Pat, 'if he had lived until next Saturday, he would have been dead a month last Tuesday.'

MIKE went to the doctor with a bad gash on the top of his head.

'How did you get that?' the doctor asked him.

'Actually,' said Mike, 'I bit myself.'

'But you couldn't have,' said the doctor, 'it's too high up.'

'I stood on a chair,' said Mike.

PAT was in a fit of depression and one night Bridget came home to find him standing on a chair with a rope around his waist.

'What the hell are you doing?' she asked him.

'I'm committing suicide,' replied Pat.

'Then why haven't you got the rope around your neck?'

'Well, I had,' said Pat, 'but it was choking me.'

WHEN Bridget's father died she went to the undertakers to buy a shroud.

'How much are the shrouds?' she asked the man behind the counter.

'Ten pounds, madam,' he replied.

'Ten pounds!' she said in disgust. 'I can get one for five pounds down town.'

'Those are of inferior quality, madam,' said the man, 'the corpse would have his knees through it in a week.'

BRIDGET and all her family were strong Catholics. She used to say that she would rather die than be buried in a Protestant graveyard.

PAT was in the army but ran away in the heat of battle and was charged with desertion. At his trial he defended himself by saying, 'I'd prefer to be a coward for five minutes than a corpse for the rest of my life.'

WHEN Bridget's brother was missing at sea, presumed drowned, she was asked to give a description in order to help with identification of the body if and when it turned up. All she could remember was that he spoke with a pronounced stutter.

AN undertaker was in the neighbourhood to collect a client but by mistake knocked on Pat's door.

'Can I help you, sir?' asked Pat.

'I hope so,' said the undertaker. 'Is this where the man that's dead lives?'

PAT once attended a public hanging. As the condemned man began to climb the rickety stairs leading to the gallows, he asked, 'Are these stairs safe?'

PAT and Bridget were once involved in a motor accident and Bridget lay sprawling across the back seat roaring with pain.

'Be quiet,' said Pat, 'you'd think there was nobody killed except yourself.'

PAT'S father was treated by the doctor for years for gout but just as the treatment had taken effect he died of a heart attack. The doctor consoled his widow by saying, 'At least you have the consolation of knowing he died fully cured.'

'WASN'T it very sad about Frank O'Sullivan,' said Pat to Mike one day.

'What happened to him?' asked Mike.

'He died in hospital,' said Pat, 'after an unsuccessful suicide attempt.'

'I'VE heard that the town's oldest resident is dead,' said Bridget to Pat one evening.

'I've heard that fellow's death reported so often and found the reports to be false that I won't believe it unless I hear it from his own lips,' replied Pat.

PAT went to the undertaker to enquire about the cost of a funeral. When told the figure he said to the undertaker, 'That's more than £500 up on last year.'

'I know,' said the undertaker, 'but you must remember that the cost of living is going up all the time.'

A FRIEND of Pat's, one of a pair of identical twins, had just died. Pat went along to sympathise with the surviving twin and said to him, 'I'm sorry for your troubles, tell me, was it you or your brother that died?'

BRIDGET looked up from her newspaper one evening and asked Pat, 'What are posthumous works, Pat? It says here that the posthumous works of this author are selling very well.'

Pat smiled indulgently at his wife's ignorance.

'Posthumous works, Bridget,' he told her, 'are works a man writes after he's dead.'

BRIDGET was once feeling so ill she declared, 'If only I could drop dead now I'd be the happiest woman alive.'

PAT'S son was a chronic medical student. One evening he came home and announced proudly to his father, 'After all those years practising on models, at last they've given me a real live corpse to work on.'

PAT and Mike were walking in a graveyard when they saw a tombstone which read:

IN LOVING MEMORY OF DAN O'HARA
WHO DIED IN AMERICA

'That's funny,' said Pat, 'I could have sworn that Dan O'Hara died before he went to America.'

MICK was on a very stormy sea voyage and feeling very seasick.

'Don't worry,' said the captain, 'you'll live,'

'Don't say that,' said Mick, 'it's only the thought of dying that's keeping me alive.'

PAT was lying in his coffin and a neighbour remarked on how well he looked.

'So he should,' said Bridget, 'he was jogging ten miles a day.'

MIKE decided that he would be cremated because he heard that undertakers were charging the earth for burials.

PAT, however, was dead against cremation. He was afraid that the crematorium might catch fire and everybody would be burned to death.

A MAN in Bridget's village had been ill from heart disease for many years. Finally, he caught a chill and died within a few days.

'At least,' Bridget consoled his widow, 'he didn't die of anything serious.'

Epitaphs

HERE lies the body of Thomas Murphy
who was lost at sea and never found
had he lived he would have been buried here.

THIS stone was erected to the memory of Din Joe O'Connell who was drowned in the Lakes of Killarney by a few of his dearest friends.

IN loving memory of John O'Donoghue who was fatally burned by an explosion of a lamp filled with Murphy's non-explosive burning fluid.

HERE lies the body of Lt. Col. MacMahon, accidentally shot by his batman while cleaning his rifle. Well done thou good and faithful servant.

ERECTED to the memory of John Burkley, accidentally shot as a mark of affection by his brother.

14

— 2 —
TRANSPORTS OF DELIGHT

THE Irish have always been a wandering people, so naturally they have a great interest in transport and locomotion. As any foreign industrialist knows the Irish have a healthy contempt for timetables, schedules and deadlines, and once again the static nature of language is not capable of coping with these rapidly changing situations.

PAT was late for work one morning, so the excuse he gave to the boss was that the train was late.

'Next time the train is late,' said the boss, 'come on the earlier train.'

PAT and Bridget went on a round-the-world cruise last year. Next year they hope to go somewhere else.

MIKE went into the big city and was looking for a shop in which to buy a pair of braces.

'Where is the braces shop, sir, please?' he asked a passerby.

'On the other side of the street,' he was told, so he crossed the road and addressed himself to a policeman.

'Excuse me, sir,' said Mick, 'where is the other side of the street?'

'It's over there,' said the policeman, pointing across the street.

'That's funny,' said Mick, 'I was over there and someone told me it was over here.'

PAT once got a job as a deep-sea diver. One day he got the following message on his headphones – come up immediately, we're sinking.

WHEN Mike was working with the railways he was heard to make the following announcements.
THE TEN O'CLOCK TRAIN LEFT AT HALF-NINE AND THERE WILL BE NO LAST TRAIN TONIGHT. THE REAR PORTION OF THE TRAIN WILL NOT RUN TONIGHT.
    THIS TRAIN STOPS NOWHERE.
When asked by a woman when was the next train for Dublin leaving, Pat replied, 'The next train for Dublin has just left.'

PAT was insuring his car against fire and the insurance agent asked him if he would like to insure it against theft as well.
    'Don't be daft,' said Pat, 'nobody would ever steal a burning car.'

PAT and Bridget were shopping in a big store when they became separated. Bridget went to the information desk and asked the girl there if she had seen a man wandering around without a woman looking like her.

PAT and Bridget were on a holiday in the Tropics and on their first night there was a violent storm.
    'I didn't sleep a single wink last night with all that thunder,' confessed Bridget the next morning.

'Why didn't you wake me?' said Pat. 'You know I can't sleep when there's thunder.'

MIKE had the following advice for motorists on narrow country roads – the best way to pass a herd of cows on the road is to keep behind them.

PAT had just arrived in England and wanted to send a telegram to inform Bridget that he had got there safely.

'How much for a telegram?' he asked the clerk.

'£5 for the telegram,' said the clerk, 'and £5 for delivery.'

'I'll just pay for the telegram,' said Pat, 'and I'll save on the delivery charge by sending her a letter telling her to come and collect the telegram.'

PAT was walking home one evening carrying a large sheet of glass when a policeman began to eye him suspiciously.

'Where did you get that?' he asked.

'I found it,' said Pat, 'it fell off the back of a lorry.'

SIGN seen on a Cork street:
THIS STREET IS A ONE WAY CUL-DE-SAC AT BOTH ENDS.

WHEN the new fire engine arrived in the village, the Council were looking for suggestions as to what might be done with the old engine.

'Why not,' suggested Pat, 'keep the old one for false alarms?'

BRIDGET was in the big city travelling by bus and wasn't too sure where she should get off.

'Where's the stop for the zoo?' she asked a woman sitting beside her on the bus.

'Watch me,' said the woman, 'and get off three stops before I do.'

PAT went to the filling station and told the lad there to put ten gallons of petrol in his tank. After a few minutes the lad came round to the front of the car and said to him, 'I'm afraid it will only hold nine and a half gallons. Would you like to drive round for a few minutes so I that I can fit the other half gallon in?'

MICK was not a great traveller. As he said himself, he only went to London once and then he only got as far as Dublin.

THERE was a crash on the old single-line West Clare Railway and Pat was reading the official regulations to see what the legal position was. At last he found the relevant paragraph and it read as follows:

'If two trains approach each other on the same track then neither shall proceed until the other has got off the track and given way to it.'

PAT and Mike were on a long country walk and were getting a bit tired.

'How far is it back to town?' they asked an old man leaning over a fence.

'Ten miles exactly,' said the man.

'Great,' said Pat to Mike, 'that's just five miles each.'

PAT and Bridget were once flying home from London when their plane caught fire. Bridget became hysterical but Pat comforted her by saying, 'Don't worry, girl, the fire isn't in our half of the plane.'

PAT and Mick were once climbing a big mountain. About halfway up they became very tired and thirsty. 'I'll tell you what,' said Pat, 'let's go down to that pub at the bottom, and we can climb the other half tomorrow.'

PAT was travelling by train when he realised that that particular train did not stop at his little home town. So he called one of the ticket checkers on the train and asked him, 'Could we stop long enough for me to run home and tell Bridget I'm being carried through.'

PAT was asking a young lad who lived near him how many miles he cycled to school.
  'Ten miles a day, sir,' answered the lad, 'five miles to school and five miles home again.'
  'That's a lot of cycling,' commented Pat, 'six schooldays in the week, so that's sixty miles a week. No, hold on, Saturday is only a half day, so it's only fifty-five miles in all – a bit better than I thought.'

MIKE once got a job as cabin-boy on a ship. As the ship was about to sail the captain asked him to go below and fetch a jar of beer.
  'No, I will not,' said Mick, 'if I did that the ship might sail without me.'

PAT was explaining to his employer why he was so late for work.
  'The bus I came in,' he told him, 'was full so I had to walk.'

BRIDGET once took up jogging and attempted to run around the Phoenix Park. About three-quarters of the way around, however, she got tired and thought she wouldn't make it, so she jogged back again.

MIKE'S son decided to hitchhike to Dublin, so he got up and made an early start to avoid all the traffic.

IRISH Railway announcement: 'There will be no trains running between Limerick and Mallow on Sunday next and delays of up to thirty minutes can be expected.'

PAT and Mike were out boating when their boat sprang a large leak. Immediately, Pat punched another hole in the boat saying, 'This will let it out.'
  All the time Mike was smiling because it wasn't leaking at his end of the boat.

AN Irish petrol company once made the following announcement:
  'If all the other petrol companies stopped giving free gifts, we would be the first to stop. As it is, we must reluctantly continue.'

MIKE once got a job driving a snowplough but refused to take it out because the weather was so bad.

PAT was working on the railway line when suddenly a train came speeding towards him along the track. He took off down the line but of course he was knocked down by the train and badly injured. When he woke up in hospital, his friend Mike asked him why he hadn't run up the bank at the side of the track.

'Don't be a fool,' said Pat, 'if I couldn't beat it on the flat, what chance had I running up a slope?'

PAT was boasting about the new Rolls-Royce he had bought.

'When the engine is running at full throttle,' he declared, 'the only sound you can hear is complete silence.'

MIKE travelled to London but was disgusted to find that nobody there had ever heard of him.

'Why, back in Ireland,' he exclaimed, 'I'm world famous.'

— 3 —

NOTICES AND HEADLINES

THE *language of notices, headlines and telegrams is condensed, perhaps too condensed at times, and inevitably ambiguity arises. The phenomenon is a worldwide one, but as usual the Irish examples are funnier, more ingenious and more ludicrous, all the more so because they are authentic.*

NOTICE in a confectioner's shop:
THE PENNY BUNS HAVE BEEN INCREASED FROM
10p TO 20p.

ADVERTISEMENT in an Irish newspaper:
PASSPORT FOR SALE, NEVER USED, OWNER
GOING ABROAD.

SIGN on an Irish shop:
CLOSED ON ACCOUNT OF RE-OPENING.

NOTICE in a shop:
DON'T BE CHEATED ELSEWHERE – COME IN
HERE.

NOTICE in a psychiatric hospital:
WE'RE ALL HERE BECAUSE WE'RE NOT ALL
THERE.

SIGN seen in a home laundry in Tralee:
WHY KILL YOURSELF WITH WASHING?
LET US DO IT BY HAND.

NOTICE reported in a Galway beauty shop:
EARS PIERCED WHILE YOU WAIT
PAY FOR TWO AND GET ONE DONE FREE

SIGN in an optician's window:
IF YOU CAN'T SEE THIS NOTICE COME INSIDE
AT ONCE – YOU MAY NEED SPECTACLES.

SIGN seen on a Limerick barber's window:
OUR HAIR RESTORER IS SO POWERFUL – THE
LESS YOU USE OF IT THE BETTER IT IS.

ROAD sign seen near Killarney:
THIS IS THE WRONG ROAD TO DUBLIN
DO NOT TAKE THIS ROAD.

MANY Irish dance halls display the following sign over
the exit:
ENTRANCE OUT

THE General Post Office in Cork had for many years a
postbox displaying the following notice:
FOR LETTERS TOO LATE FOR THE NEXT
DELIVERY.

NOTICE on a well-known Cork publisher's door:
GONE TO LUNCH – BACK IN AN HOUR.
ALREADY GONE HALF AN HOUR.

SIGN in a shop in Dundalk:
VISIT OUR BARGAIN BASEMENT ON THE THIRD
FLOOR.

NEWSPAPER headline:
MAN STATED TO BE CRITICAL FOLLOWING
FATAL ACCIDENT

NEWSPAPER headline:
POPE DIES FOR SECOND TIME IN A MONTH

SIGN on an Irish garage:
LAST PETROL STATION UNTIL THE NEXT ONE

THE following notice was displayed for many years on Sligo jail:
ALL PRISONERS NOT BACK IN JAIL BY 11 P.M. SHARP WILL BE LOCKED OUT FOR THE NIGHT.

NEWSPAPER headline in 1986:
PRICELESS IRISH CHALICE WORTH £5.5M

SIGN in an Irish auctioneers:
THE HIGHEST BIDDER TO BE THE PURCHASER – UNLESS SOMEBODY BIDS MORE

NOTICE in a Tipperary shop:
NO DISSATISFIED CUSTOMER IS EVER ALLOWED TO LEAVE THIS SHOP.

THE following notice stood for many years on the banks of the River Shannon:
WHEN THIS NOTICE IS UNDER WATER IT IS UNSAFE TO CROSS THE RIVER AT THIS POINT

SIGN seen at a country race meeting:
DONKEY RACES OPEN TO RESIDENTS OF THE PARISH ONLY

NOTICE seen on a shop in Donegal:
YES WE ARE OPEN – PLEASE CALL BACK AT SOME OTHER TIME

NEWSPAPER headline:
BODY OF MAN FOUND IN GRAVEYARD

NEWSPAPER advertisement:
GENUINE ANTIQUES FOR SALE – AS NEW

NOTICE on tip head:
NO DUMPING ALLOWED BY ORDER

NOTICE in a hotel:
PLEASE DO NOT SWITCH ON TELEVISION
EXCEPT WHEN IN USE.

NOTICE in a golf club near Cork:
TROUSERS MAY NOW BE WORN BY LADIES ON
THE COURSE – BUT THEY MUST BE REMOVED
BEFORE ENTERING THE CLUBHOUSE

SIGN in a Belfast post office:
PENS WILL NOT BE PROVIDED UNTIL PEOPLE
STOP TAKING THEM AWAY

SIGN in a Roscommon barber shop:
SPECIAL OFFER: HAIRCUTS 50p ALL THIS WEEK.
ONE PER CUSTOMER ONLY.

SIGN on a Wicklow church:
CLOSED ON SUNDAYS

NOTICE on a Carlow restaurant:
SORRY – WE ARE CLOSED FOR LUNCH

NEWSPAPER headline:
PASSENGERS HIT BY CANCELLED TRAINS

NOTICE in a restaurant:
CUSTOMERS WHO THINK OUR WAITRESSES ARE
RUDE SHOULD SEE THE MANAGER

NOTICE on a Galway dance hall:
DISCO ON SUNDAY NIGHT. VERY EXCLUSIVE.
EVERYBODY WELCOME

NOTICE in a cemetery:
YOU ARE ALLOWED TO PICK FLOWERS ONLY
OFF YOUR OWN GRAVE

NOTICE on a Dublin shop:
OPEN 24 HOURS A DAY
LONGER AT WEEKENDS

NOTICE in a Kilkenny chemist's:
WE DISPENSE WITH ACCURACY

SIGN on a Clare dance hall:
LADIES   AND   GENTLEMEN   WELCOME
REGARDLESS OF SEX

INSCRIPTION on a box of string:
FOR BITS OF STRING TOO SHORT TO BE OF ANY
USE

— 4 —
FOOD AND LIQUOR

THE Irish are renowned for their drinking habits throughout the world – but they only drink to forget the fact that they are alcoholics. In between drinks they are also known to eat from time to time, though an Irishman will never eat on an empty stomach. In general, he likes to combine both activities by drinking a certain potent black beverage because 'there's eatin' and drinkin' in it'.

BRIDGET keeps hoping that some day scientists will find a cure for wheatgerm.

WHEN Mike ate fish he always ate herrings. 'Herrings are the freshest of all fish,' he used to declare, 'because the herring lives longer after it's dead than any other creature.'

PAT walked into a bar and asked for a whiskey and ice.
  'I'm sorry, sir,' said the barman, 'we have no ice.'
  'I'll have a whiskey and water then,' said Pat.
  'Sorry, sir,' said the barman, 'all our water is frozen.'

'LET'S go to McCarthy's Restaurant,' said Pat to Bridget one evening.
  'No,' said Bridget, 'let's go somewhere else. That place is so crowded, no one goes there any longer.'

PAT and Mike went picking blackberries.

'How will I know the ones that are ripe?' Mike asked.

'That's easy,' said Pat, 'the blackberry is the only fruit that's red when it's green.'

'JUST how drunk were you?' the judge asked Mike, after a policeman had given evidence that Mike had refused to walk a white line without a safety net.

'I was as drunk as a judge,' said Mike.

'Surely you mean as drunk as a lord,' said the judge.

'Yes, my lord,' said Mike.

'Look,' said the judge, 'stop fooling about, how drunk were you?'

'I was sober enough to know I was drunk,' said Mike.

Helplessly, the judge asked the policeman to continue his evidence on Mike's condition.

'He was speechless drunk, your honour,' said the policeman, 'and using foul, obscene and insulting language.'

DURING the dreadful famine of 1846, a relief worker was bringing food to a starving family in a remote Irish village.

'Thank God for the famine,' said one old man, 'if it wasn't for it, sure we'd all starve to death.'

'WHY are you eating so fast?' Bridget once asked one of her children.

'I want to finish my meal,' said the little lad, 'before I lose my appetite.'

PAT once opened a bakery shop. He used to sell a bread so light that a pound of it weighed only twelve ounces.

BRIDGET was asked to describe what it was like when Pat had one of his massive hangovers.

'Well,' she said, 'the morning after, I bring him up the newspaper and he reads the obituary column. Then, if he's not in it, he gets up.'

MIKE came home from the pub one night to find his house empty and all the doors locked. Finally he broke in through a window and found the following note from his wife on the table: 'Your salad is in the oven and you'll find the key of the door under the mat.'

MIKE was out on a drinking spree one night and left his umbrella behind in one of the pubs he visited. Next day he went to nine of the pubs and failed to find his umbrella, but in the tenth one it turned up.

'Do you know what I'm going to tell you,' he said to the barman over a celebratory pint, 'you're the only honest barman in town. All the others said they hadn't got it.'

BRIDGET once left the following note for the milkman:

'Two pints of milk today, By today I mean tomorrow as I wrote it yesterday.'

MIKE and his friends went into a pub and found a nice quiet corner. Mike went over to the bar and ordered twenty pints of beer.

'Would you like a tray, sir?' asked the barman.

'Certainly not,' said Mike, 'haven't I enough to carry with all these drinks?'

PAT went into the illicit liquor business making illegal poteen. When he took his stuff into town to sell, he always drove his donkey cart very slowly. It wasn't because he was afraid of the police – he just wanted to give it a chance to age a bit.

MIKE was staying in a little country hotel and was wandering about early in the morning. The landlord said to him, 'I'm sorry, sir, the bar won't be open for another hour, but would you like a drink while you're waiting?'

A BEGGAR once called at Bridget's door and told her that he had just sold his last saucepan in order to buy some porridge to cook in it.

PAT was once describing a recipe for Bridget's soup.
'She takes a pint of water,' he said, 'and boils it down to make it strong.'

MIKE was explaining to his wife why the meat he had just bought from the butcher didn't taste very good.
'It comes from cattle that are killed after they died,' he explained.

BRIDGET was getting a bit fed up because for three days in a row the milk had gone sour, yet she didn't want to offend the milkman by mentioning the fact.
'If I were you,' said Pat, 'I'd take the bull by the horns and demand fresh milk.'

ADVERTISEMENT in an Irish Newspaper: 'For sale, a quantity of port drunk by Queen Victoria on her visit to Dublin.'

PAT once bought a cow from a man because he told him that it would give milk indefinitely without having a calf. 'It's in her blood,' he assured him, 'because she came of a cow that never had a calf.'

PAT and Mike were once the worse for drink.
  'Do you remember your man Frank Murphy?' asked Pat.
  'What's his name again?' asked Mike.
  'Who?' asked Pat.

BRIDGET was put on a severe diet but her doctor was amazed to see her in a restaurant tucking into bacon, cabbage and potatoes.
  'What about your diet, Bridget?' he asked her.
  'Oh, I've had my diet,' said Bridget, 'now I'm having my dinner.'

MIKE was asked what was his favourite drink.
  'The next one,' he replied.

PAT and Mike were staying in a hotel a bit the worse for drink. They fused all the lights in the hotel playing a game. The object of the game was to turn out the light quickly enough so they could see what the dark looked like.

— 5 —

MEDICINE AND THE BODY

PAT'S *father used to follow the medical profession – he was an undertaker. Most Irishmen and Irishwomen believe that what doctors preach is a load of bull anyway and that anyone who has the energy to visit a doctor isn't really ill in the first place. As for psychiatrists, it was that honorary Irishman, Sam Goldwyn, who first coined the immortal phrase, 'Anyone who goes to see a psychiatrist should have his head examined.'*

An Irishman's body has wittily been defined as 'merely a machine for turning potatoes into human nature', and it doesn't take too much imagination to come up with a liquid equivalent.

PAT was explaining to Mike how nature sometimes compensates for deficiencies of the body.

'For example,' he told him, 'if someone has weak eyesight, he may have good hearing to compensate for his deficiency, or if he has poor hearing, he may have a good sense of smell,'

'I think I see what you're getting at,' said Mike at last, 'I've often noticed myself that if a fellow has one short leg, the other one is always a little bit longer.'

PAT was warned about the smells coming from his drains so he wrote to the local council asking them to come and investigate.

The council officer replied that there was no point in doing this as it was the smell you couldn't smell at all that did you the most harm.

MIKE went to the doctor who gave him some pills to take.

'Are these habit forming?' Mike asked him.

'Certainly not,' said the doctor, 'I've been taking them myself every day for the last twenty years and I can assure you they are not habit forming.'

PAT went to the doctor who prescribed suppositories. When he returned a few weeks later the doctor asked him if the treatment had worked.

'Not a bit,' said Pat. 'I ate about a dozen of them and for all the good they did me I might as well have stuck them in my rear end.'

WHEN Bridget was a nurse, one of her principal tasks was waking up patients to give them their sleeping pills.

'LEARN to cut your fingernails with your left hand,' Pat's father used to advise him, 'in case you lose your right hand.'

MIKE had a large bald patch so he used to wear a wig with a large bald patch on the top. He figured that that way nobody would realise he was wearing a wig.

PAT was telling Mike that when he was born he weighed only a few ounces.

'Wow,' said Mike, 'that's almost incredible, tell me, did you live?'

'Live?' chuckled Pat. 'Boy, you ought to see me now.'

BRIDGET was once being examined by her optician.

'Now shut your eyes,' he told her, 'and look at me.'

PAT was once prescribed an emetic by his doctor, but try as he liked, he couldn't keep it in his stomach.

PAT was once at death's door but the doctor pulled him through.

MIKE was talking about certain tablets he was taking and on which his life depended.

'They are vital for my continued existence,' he claimed. 'Even if I didn't need them, I'd still have to take them.'

PAT was very ill indeed so Bridget sent for the doctor. After a brief examination the doctor announced that Pat was dead.

'I'm not,' cried Pat feebly from his bed.

'Be quiet,' said Bridget, 'do you know better than the doctor?'

MIKE went to the doctor and told him he was suffering from hallucinations.

'Nonsense, man,' said the doctor, 'you're just imagining things.'

BRIDGET was in a shoe shop and had tried on over a hundred pairs of shoes.

'I'm sorry,' she apologised to the assistant, 'the trouble is that one of my feet is bigger than the other.'

'Not at all madam,' said the placatory assistant, 'it's smaller if anything.'

MIKE was badly injured in a shooting accident and the doctor reported on his four wounds as follows: 'The first two wounds are fatal all right, but the third and fourth are not and with good care and attention the patient should recover soon.'

BRIDGET once passed a blind man sitting at a street corner, so, feeling sorry for him she threw tenpence into his box.

'That's a bit mean,' said the blind man at once, 'tenpence from a lady of means like yourself.'

'If you're blind,' retorted Bridget, 'how did you know it was tenpence I put in?'

'Actually,' said the man, 'I'm only sitting in for the regular blind man because it's his afternoon off – he's gone to the movies.'

PAT was attending a psychiatrist for a nervous complaint but when he found out that the fee was £50 per visit he told the shrink that he didn't want any more treatment.

'If you think you're leaving here cured after only one visit you're crazy,' said the psychiatrist.

— 6 —
JURIES AND THE LAW

WHAT is it about jury service, courtrooms or any brush with the law that brings out the very worst in us and makes the sanest of people become gibbering idiots? Irish courtrooms and evidence given by Irish men and women throughout recorded history have been full of the most delicious blunders, lies and inconsistencies imaginable.

MIKE was involved in a law case and was unfortunate enough to hire a solicitor notorious for his high fees. On his final bill there were the following items:
Item: To crossing the street to discuss your case with you
      – 5 guineas.
Item: To re-crossing the street after discovering it wasn't you – 5 guineas.

PAT was tried by jury charged with stealing a horse. After a few hours of listening to boring evidence, however, he suddenly pleaded guilty. The judge instructed the jury to find him guilty, but to his amazement they retired for over an hour and returned a unanimous verdict of 'not guilty'. The judge protested that the defendant had pleaded guilty, but the foreman of the jury explained: 'You don't know him like we do, your honour. He's the biggest liar in the entire country and you can't believe a word he says.'

PAT was once convicted of a serious crime and just after sentence had been passed he confessed that he had actually been in jail when the crime was committed.

'Why on earth didn't you tell the court that?' his lawyer asked.

'I thought it might prejudice the jury against me,' said Pat.

PAT was called for service as a juryman in a major murder trial. However, he was challenged and asked, 'Do you believe in capital punishment?'

'Yes,' said Pat, 'if it's not too severe.'

A FARMER who heard a lot of noise coming from his chicken coop one night suspected burglars. So he went downstairs with his gun and shouted out, 'Is there anyone in there?'

Back came a squeaky voice, 'There's no one in here except us chickens.'

'That's all right,' said the farmer, 'but I could have sworn I heard a noise.'

PAT was charged with poaching a pair of rabbits. In defence he stated that the field from which he took them was 'alive with dead rabbits'.

'ARE you innocent or guilty?' Bridget was asked in a court case.

'How can I tell,' asked Bridget, 'until I have heard the evidence?'

BRIDGET was charged with reckless driving and causing the death of no less than twenty-four pigs. The prosecuting counsel was rubbing in the charges and emphasising the magnitude of the crime.

'Twenty-four pigs,' he thundered, 'twice the number in the jury box.'

'WHEN I sit on the bench,' an Irish judge is once said to have remarked, 'I promise to be neither partial nor impartial.'

Some Irish Jury Verdicts

WE find the man who stole the mare, not guilty.

WE are unanimous – nine to three.

WE find the defendant not guilty but recommend he does not do it again.

WE recommend that the defendant be hanged and we hope it will be a lesson to him.

WE find this man not guilty if he promises to give the money back.

WE are of one mind – insane.

WE find the defendant guilty of innocently committing perjury.

WE return a verdict of guilty against the unknown murderer who fired the alleged shot which killed O'Hara.

WE the jury have good friends on both sides of this case and would prefer not to get involved.

BRIDGET once did jury service in a murder trial and the defending lawyer addressed the jury thus: 'Ladies and gentlemen of the jury, think of the accused's mother, his only mother.'

IN another case, Mike accused the police of brutality claiming that he had been handcuffed by the feet.

PAT and Mike were escaping from jail and were being followed by the police with tracker dogs. They decided to climb into two trees to evade capture. As the dogs came sniffing to the base of Pat's tree, he went 'miaow, miaow'.

'Come away from that tree,' said the policeman to the dog, 'that's only a cat up there.'

Then the dog began to sniff at the base of Mike's tree.

'Moo, moo,' went Mike.

PAT was up in court charged with bankruptcy. The judge asked him if he could pay anything at all towards the settlement that had been awarded against him.

'Not a penny, your honour,' said Pat. 'Everything I own I've given to my lawyer and three of the jury.'

MIKE was charged with stealing a goat but the judge told him that he was acquitted.

'Acquitted,' said Mike, 'what does that mean? Does it mean I can keep the goat?'

PAT was charged with stealing horses and the judge told him that he could be tried by the judge himself or by a jury of his peers.

'What do you mean by "peers"?' asked Pat.

'Men and women,' said the judge, 'of your own class and equal.'

'Try me yourself, judge,' said Pat, 'I don't want to be tried by a bunch of horse thieves.'

MIKE was charged with attempted murder because he threatened a woman with a knife.

'I didn't really intend to murder her, your honour,' he told the judge, 'I just meant to frighten her to death.'

'YOU are charged,' said the judge to Pat, 'with having wilfully, feloniously and with malice aforethought appropriated to your own use and behoof a certain article, to wit, a bovine quadruped – the aforementioned quadruped having been wrongfully and feloniously abstracted by you from the estate of one Daniel Murphy on or about the fourth day of July Anno Domini 1987 contrary to the law of the land. How do you plead?'

'Not guilty, your honour,' said Pat. 'Sure all I did was steal a cow.'

'YOU leave this court,' said the judge to Mike, 'with no other stain on your character than the fact that you were acquitted by a Limerick jury.'

Some Irish Wills

I LEAVE everything to the doctor who pulls me through my final illness.

I LEAVE my entire fortune for medical research in the hope that after I am dead a cure will be found for the disease from which I have died so that I can be cured and live to spend the money.

... AND finally to my no-good brother-in-law, Sean whom I promised to mention in my will – hello there, Sean.

AN Irish farmer was settling his affairs with his solicitor. 'To each of my five sons I leave £50,000 and to each of my seven daughters I leave £30,000,' he said to the furiously typing solicitor.

'Hold on a moment,' said the solicitor, 'that comes to nearly half a million pounds, and you have assets of only £500. Where is all this money to come from?'

'Blast them,' said the farmer, 'let them work for it like I did.'

OLD Irish proverb: 'Where there's a will, there are relatives.'

— 7 —
THE JARVEY AND THE GILLIE

THE wit and silver tongue of the jarvey are part of Irish folklore. These fellows live off their wits, delighting tourists with their blarney, flattery spread so thick that you can see right through it. The jarvey is the direct descendant of the gillie, the man who helped out on fishing trips or with hunting parties.

Let us call our prototype jarvey or gillie Dinny, and locate him somewhere in the south-west of Ireland between Blarney and Killarney, amid lakes and jaunting cars, an unashamed chapter of stage Irishry.

DINNY was once faced with a huge crowd of tourists waiting to avail themselves of his services. He remarked, 'If they all get on this jaunting car, there will be half of them left behind.'

AN elderly American tourist once asked Dinny what age he thought she was. He replied diplomatically, 'Begor madam, whatever age you are, you don't look it.'

PASSING by the local church tower a tourist noticed that each of the three clocks showed a different time so he asked Dinny for a reason.

'If they all showed the same time,' said Dinny with perfect logic, 'then there would be need for only one clock.'

A TOURIST once asked Dinny if he spoke any other languages.

'How about Gaelic?' he questioned him. 'Can you understand Gaelic?'

'Yes,' twinkled Dinny, 'if it's spoken in English.'

'How about Esperanto?' continued the tourist.

'I speak that like a native,' retorted Dinny.

DINNY had been reading books on Geography to impress his customers.

'Say, Dinny, where did all those rocks come from?' a passenger asked him one day.

'Those rocks,' said Dinny, proud of his knowledge, 'were laid down by massive glaciers as they came down from the mountains.'

'That's pretty good,' said the tourist. 'Tell me, where are all those glaciers now?'

Dinny was perplexed, but only for a moment. 'Gone back for more rocks,' he smiled.

'WHAT'S the average tip you receive?' an English tourist, anxious to do the right thing, asked Dinny.

'Ten pounds,' said Dinny.

The tourist handed over ten pounds, feeling however that it was a bit much.

'Thank you, sir,' said Dinny, having tucked the money safely away in his pocket, 'you're the first customer I've ever had that comes up to the average.'

DINNY had taken a party of fishermen around the lakes and they had a very successful day's fishing, so they invited him into their posh hotel for a drink. In the lounge were a dozen heads of deer proudly mounted on the wall.

'What do you think of those?' Dinny was asked.

'Well,' said Dinny thoughtfully, 'that herd of deer must have been travelling at a fair old pace when they hit that wall.'

'ARE there many fish in this river?' a tourist asked Dinny.

'It's so bad,' said Dinny, 'that people can't take water out of it because of the taste of salmon in their tea.'

ANY time he saw a rainbow, Dinny used to remark to his passengers, 'The rainbow is not an optical illusion – it only looks like one.'

DINNY drove his passengers to the edge of a cliff – the highest unprotected cliff in the South of Ireland.

'Say, this looks dangerous,' said an alarmed passenger. 'How come they don't have a warning notice here?'

'They did have,' said Dinny, 'but nobody ever fell over, so they took it away.'

'THAT,' said Dinny, pointing to Carrantouhill, 'is Ireland's highest mountain.'

'Hold on,' said one of his passengers, 'that mountain beside it seems to be somewhat higher.'

'Begod you could be right,' said Dinny peering with his hand over his eyes, 'The trouble with Carrantouhill is that it's down in a hollow.'

DINNY lived in a little cottage way up in the mountains and one morning the postman arrived with a single letter for him.

'That's a long journey you had with a single letter,' said Dinny, 'you should have posted it.'

DINNY had two standard explanations to amuse his fishing clients. Firstly he claimed that pollution in the water was caused by all those dead fish swimming around, and secondly that the sea was salty because of all those herrings swimming around.

'DO you believe in ghosts?' a passenger once asked Dinny.

'Indeed I do not,' he replied, 'I've seen too many of them to believe in them.'

'MOST of the things you tell us,' one of his passengers remarked to Dinny, 'are either improbable or impossible.'

'Ireland,' said Dinny, 'is a country where the improbable frequently happens and the impossible always happens.'

'WHO lives in that fine house we're passing?' Dinny was asked.

'A man from London, who never sets foot in this place,' said Dinny. 'The whole country is crawling with absentee landlords.'

DINNY'S fishing party were on the lakes but weren't having any luck.

'Look here,' complained one of them bitterly, 'we've been on this lake for over six hours and haven't had a single bite.'

'We're not nearly as bad as last week's party,' said Dinny cheerfully, 'they were twelve hours in the boat without a single bite.'

AN Englishman came over to Killarney for a week's fishing and hired Dinny as his gillie. In the entire week, however, he caught only one salmon.

'Do you know,' he said to Dinny as he departed, 'this salmon cost me £500?'

'Weren't you lucky,' smiled Dinny, 'that you didn't catch two of them.'

DINNY once took an Indian prince on a fishing trip and the prince was lucky enough to feel a nibble on his line. Dinny's exhortations went as follows:

'Hold him, your highness, play him, your honour; give him more line, your worship; pull him in, your lordship; ah you've lost him, you foreign bastard.'

ONE of Dinny's clients hooked a very small fish only a few inches long and after a fierce battle managed to bring it to the end of his rod.

'What do I do now?' asked the helpless fisherman.

'Maybe,' smiled Dinny, 'you could take a knife, climb up the rod and stab it to death.'

'HAVE you ever read *The Penguin Book of Quotations?*' a literary client asked Dinny.

'No sir,' said Dinny, 'I didn't even know that penguins could talk.'

'DO you believe in fairies?' Dinny was asked.

'I don't,' said Dinny, 'but I know they are there and that they probably don't believe in me either.'

'HOW well do you know this lake?' a client asked Dinny while they were in a boat together.

'I know every rock in this lake,' said Dinny. There followed a mighty crash. 'That,' said Dinny, 'was one of the biggest rocks just now.'

— 8 —
SIR BOYLE ROACH – FATHER OF THE HERD

SIR Boyle Roach is generally acknowledged to be the finest proponent of Irish wit and wisdom – and he sired many a fine 'Irish bull'. Born in 1743, he was a member of the Irish Parliament for the district of Tralee in 1775. So many bulls have been attributed to him that he couldn't possibly have had time to litter them all. There are some who claim that Boyle Roach's speeches were written for him by others and that he delivered his speeches without notes and so recalled the words rather than the sense. Others claim that he was a wily old gentleman whose 'bulls' were quite deliberate and made in order to draw attention to himself. Whatever the truth of the matter, here are a few of the best:

'SINGLE misfortunes rarely come alone and the worst of all misfortunes is usually followed by a greater misfortune.'

'THE only way of preventing what is past is to put a stop to it before it happens.'

BOYLE Roach accused an opposition member of being the sort of man who would pat you on the back in front of your face but who would stab you in the chest once your back was turned.

'MR Speaker, the country is in such a desperate state that little children, who can neither walk nor talk, are running around the street cursing the maker.'

'I ANSWER in the affirmative with an emphatic "NO!"'

'I WOULD give up half – nay, the whole of the constitution to preserve the remainder.'

SIR Boyle once proposed that all wooden gates in Ireland should be made of iron.

ON another occasion, Sir Boyle Roach declared that the tax on leather would be severely felt by the barefooted peasantry of Ireland. 'But,' he continued, 'this situation could easily be remedied by making the under-leathers of wood.'

IN 1784 the Parliament of which Sir Boyle was a member introduced a bill containing the following clause:
  'If a member is unable to write, he may authorise another person to frank for him, provided that on the back of the letter so franked the member gives a certificate under his hand of his inability to write.'

'THE people of this country are living from hand to mouth like the birds of the air.'

'THE cup of Ireland's miseries has been overflowing for centuries, but it is not yet full.'

'MANY hundreds of people were destitute even of the very goods they possessed.'

IN opposing certain reforms in the legal system Boyle Roach said, 'By trial by jury I have lived, and please God with trial by jury I shall die.'

'THREE-quarters of what the opposition say about us is lies and the other half is without any foundation in truth.'

'THE only living beasts on the farms of Ireland are the birds that fly over them.'

LETTER written by Sir Boyle Roach during the Irish rebellion.

Dear Sir,

Having now a little peace and quiet, I sit down to inform you of the bustle and confusion we are in from the bloodthirsty rebels, many of whom are now, thank God, killed and dispersed. To give you some idea of the danger we are in, I will only say that while I am writing this letter I have a sword in one hand and a pistol in the other. We are in a pretty mess; can get nothing to eat, and no wine to drink except whiskey. When we sit down to dinner we are obliged to keep both hands armed. I concluded from the beginning that this would be the end; and I am right, for it is not half over yet. At present there are such goings on that everything is at a standstill. I should have answered your letter a fortnight ago, but I only received it this morning; indeed, hardly a mail arrives safe without being robbed. No longer ago than yesterday the mail coach from Dublin was robbed near this town; the bags had been judiciously left behind for fear of accident, and by great good luck there was nobody in the coach except two outside passengers, who had nothing for the thieves to take. Last Thursday an alarm was given that a gang of rebels, in full retreat from Drogheda, were advancing under the French standard; but they had no colours, nor any drums except bagpipes. Immediately every man in the place, including women and children, ran out to meet them. We soon found our forces a great deal too little, and were far too near to think of retreating. Death was in every face, and to it we went. By the time half our party were killed we began to be all alive. Fortunately the rebels had no guns, except pistols, cutlasses, and pikes; and we had plenty of muskets and ammunition. We put them all to the sword; not a soul of them escaped alive except some that were drowned in the adjoining bog. In fact, in a short time nothing was heard but silence. Their uniforms were all different – chiefly green. After the action was over we went to rummage their camp. All we found was a few pikes without heads, a parcel of empty bottles filled with water, and a bundle of blank French commissions filled up with Irish names. Troops are now stationed round, which exactly squares with my ideas of security. Adieu. I have only time to add, that I am yours in haste, B.R. P.S. If you do not receive this, of course it must have miscarried; therefore I beg you write and let me know.

— 9 —

THE FAMILY

WHERE *there is some important human activity or institution there will be jokes, and the Irish family is no exception — children, parents, relations and in-laws all grab part of the action. Pat and Bridget are of course man and wife and Mike is almost part of the family.*

WHEN Pat and Bridget's first baby was born, the first question Mike asked was, 'Is it a boy or a child?'

PAT and Bridget had twin boys and she was asked how she could tell them apart. She replied, 'I stick my finger in Tim's mouth and if he bites me I know it's Frank. Anyway, Tim is an identical twin but Frank isn't.'

Asked if the twins cried at night, she replied, 'Each of them cries so loud you can't hear the other.'

MIKE was asked if he had any photographs of himself as a baby. He said that he hadn't but that he was going to have one taken.

PAT was philosophising about the terrible state of the world.

'The happiest man,' he declared, 'is the man who has

never been born. But such is the nature of life that this is a privilege granted only to one in a million.'

MIKE told a friend that he hadn't got a living relative in the world except for a cousin who died in America three years ago.

BRIDGET wrote to all her relatives in November, explaining that because of the postal expense she wouldn't be sending them any Christmas greetings this year.

EVERY year Pat threw a huge family party that went on and on and on. In fact nobody ever went home until everyone else was gone.

PAT complained that Bridget was a poor housekeeper and spent very little time in the house. 'In fact,' he declared, 'for every time she comes in, she goes out three times.'

PAT and Bridget hired a babysitter for their little boy but she couldn't keep him quiet unless she let him make a noise. She complained that baby was good only when he was being naughty.

AFTER Pat died, Bridget decided that she would like to have a nice photograph to remember him by, but the only one she could find had him wearing a loud and vulgar cap. She took the photograph to a professional photographer and asked him if he could remove the cap and touch up the photograph.

'Certainly,' he replied, 'I'll do that. Tell me, which side did he part his hair on?'

'Won't you see that when you take his cap off?' said Bridget.

MIKE was seen wearing a new suit one morning and a friend asked why. 'Well,' he replied, 'I'm loading a cart of manure this morning and I'm getting married this afternoon. I'll save time because I'll only have to change my vest and underwear.'

WHEN the family squabbles got too much for her, Bridget used to say to Pat, 'Happy are the parents who have no children.'

AFTER Pat was away from home for three years, his wife Bridget had a baby. Mike asked him if he was a bit suspicious about the happy event.

'Certainly not,' beamed Pat, 'there was five years between me and my brother.'

MIKE was very ugly, but he claimed that he had been born a very beautiful baby and a jealous nurse had exchanged him at birth.

'IS Bill a relative of yours?' Pat asked Mike.

'He's a distant relative,' said Mike, 'I was my parents' first child and he was their twelfth.'

MIKE: 'Was the latest child a boy or a girl, Pat?'
Pat: 'Have a guess, Mike.'
Mike: 'It was a girl.'

Pat: 'No, guess again.'
Mike: 'It was a boy?'
Pat: 'Ah, someone must have told you.'

WHEN Pat joined the army he forgot to take his big overcoat with him so Bridget posted it to him. To save weight, she cut off the metal buttons and put them in one of the pockets.

MIKE had a very strict father. His favourite saying to his children was, 'Silence when you speak to me.'

'THAT'S a beautiful child you have there,' said a neighbour to Bridget.

'That's nothing,' said Bridget, 'you should see his photograph.'

MICK was up in court charged, among other things, with giving a wrong name to a policeman.

'Why did you tell the policeman your name was Tom O'Sullivan, when it was Mick O'Toole?' asked the judge.

'Your honour,' Mick replied, 'my mother was married twice.'

BRIDGET never put milk in the fridge as soon as it was delivered – she always gave the fridge some time to warm up first.

PAT described a woman he met as 'the ugliest woman in the world'. The woman's sister called round and threatened to sue him if he did not issue an immediate apology. Pat's statement read – 'Yesterday I described Miss X as the ugliest woman in the world. Now that I have seen her sister, I wish to withdraw that statement.'

MIKE was giving Pat the run of his new flat. 'Here's a key,' he told him, 'but the lock doesn't work. Neither does the bell, but if you want to get in just give the door a good kick.'

'WHO was that at the door?' Bridget asked Pat one evening after there was a knock at the door.

'Nobody,' said Pat, 'just a man looking for the wrong house.'

PAT was sitting in the bar at Shannon Airport when he got into conversation with an American.

'I've come to meet my brother,' said Pat, 'it's his first trip home from America in forty years,'

'Will you be able to recognise him?' asked the American.

'I'm sure I won't,' said Pat, 'after all those years.'

'I wonder if he will recognise you?' said the American.

'Of course he will,' said Pat, 'sure I haven't been away at all.'

BRIDGET was warning her little girl about the dangers of being molested. 'Be careful going to school,' she warned her, 'and don't speak to any strangers unless you know them.'

'WHAT is Tom's other name?' Pat asked Mike.

'Tom who?' asked Mike.

— 10 —
ACTS OF VIOLENCE AND OTHER SPORTING TALES

'THE Irish,' said Samuel Johnson, 'are fair people – they never speak well of each other.' Someone else added, 'The Irish are at peace only when they are fighting.' This reputation, it must be admitted, is probably deserved, and it has been well said that the Irish don't know what they want, but will fight like hell until they get it. That old bulldog himself, Winston Churchill, said that whenever England thought she had got the answer to the Irish question, the Irish changed the question.

In this chapter we look at the bulls involved in war and fighting and in the army, and because Irish sports fields sometimes resemble battlefields, we have included sporting bulls as well.

PAT was sleeping one night when he thought he heard a burglar in the room, so he took the shotgun that he always kept by his bedside and let fly a few rounds, narrowly missing his own toes. On getting up and finding that it was a false alarm, he exclaimed, 'Thank God I didn't have the bed turned the other way round or I would have blown my head off.'

'DO you need a police station in your village?' Mike was asked in a survey.

'No,' said Mike, 'although we have got one. But if we didn't have one, we would need one.'

BRIDGET saw a film in which there was a man lying dead with a bullet hole in the middle of his forehead.

'Wasn't it the mercy of God,' she declared, 'that it didn't go through the unfortunate man's eye.'

MIKE once boasted that he had got in free into the All-Ireland football final by bribing one of the men on the gate with £20.

MIKE'S wife wasn't happy about him joining the Army.

'If you lose both your legs in the battle,' she warned him, 'don't come running home to me.'

PAT and Mike were out hunting rabbits when they saw a fine specimen.

'Quick Mike,' said Pat, 'shoot him.'

'I can't,' said Mike, 'I've run out of ammunition.'

'Look,' said Pat, 'I know that, you know that, but the rabbit doesn't know that.'

THE sergeant told Mike to go and stand at the end of the line. Mike came back and told him there was someone standing there already.

PAT joined the 75th Regiment of the Army to be near his brother who was in the 76th Regiment.

PAT joined the Air Force and was asked to test a new type of parachute. No, it wasn't the type that opened on impact, it was the type that opened when ten feet from the ground. The theory was that if it failed to open at that height, then the jumper wouldn't have very far to fall. On Pat's first jump from 10,000 feet he didn't wear a parachute at all, because it was only a practice jump.

'THIS is a crooked card game,' remarked Mike one evening. 'Someone isn't playing the hand I dealt him.'

'WHAT'S all that noise?' Bridget asked Pat one evening.
  'It's nothing, dear,' said Pat, 'they're just forcing some men to join the Volunteers.'

Bridget once entered a competition to predict the score in the All-Ireland football final. First prize was two tickets for the match.

PAT and Mike were lying in wait one night for their sworn enemy in order to beat him to a pulp. After about three hours Pat said to Mike, 'He's late, I hope to God nothing has happened to the poor fellow.'

PAT, in his youth, was a noted football referee. He developed a new technique of having extra time before the match began in case of fog.

MIKE joined the Army but came a cropper while out drilling on the parade ground. He tripped over a hole that was sticking right up out of the ground.

PAT and Mike were having a fight and the insults began to fly. 'Say another thing like that to me,' said Pat, 'and I'll knock the brains out of your empty head.'

BRIDGET took up middle-distance running but wasn't very successful in competitions. Then after many attempts she finally won a race. 'I'm first at last,' she declared, 'I was always behind before.'

PAT and Mike were out hunting duck when Pat took a fine shot, hit a duck and it fell at their feet.

Turning to Mike, he expected a glowing compliment.

'You could have saved your shot,' said Mike casually, 'the fall would have killed it anyway.'

PAT was wearing a top hat when somebody fired a shot at him and it went right through the top of the hat. Bridget declared, 'Weren't you lucky you weren't wearing a low hat.'

'MY brother Tom,' boasted Mike, 'was the finest fighter in the country. Although he had only one arm, he used to dispose of opponents two at a time by banging their heads together.'

'I thought you said he had only one arm,' objected Pat.

'When my brother got into a fight,' said Mike, 'he forgot all about that.'

'WHY did you hit Mike?' the judge asked Pat.

'Well, your honour,' said Pat, 'I knew he was going to hit me so I retaliated first.'

PAT said that his most abiding memory of the Army was the announcement, 'Please inform the troops that communications have completely broken down.'

'WHAT struck me most about the war,' said Pat, 'was the number of bullets that missed me.'

'WHAT are you two fighting about?' a policeman asked Pat and Mike one night.

'We're not fighting,' they told him, 'we're just trying to separate ourselves from each other.'

BRIDGET fell in the kitchen one evening and Pat said to her, 'Are you hurt, my love? Come over here and let me pick you up.'

PAT was fishing and it started to rain, so he went under a bridge for shelter.

'You're not afraid of a few drops of rain are you?' Mike taunted him.

'Not at all,' said Pat, 'the fish come in here to shelter too.'

PAT was drilling a local force of volunteer soldiers.

'All of you without arms,' he ordered them, 'raise your hands.'

— 11 —

BUSINESS AND MONEY

THE Irish have a pragmatic approach to financial matters. They feel that money was made to be spent and that if you hold on to money for too long, it is inclined to burn a hole in your pocket. Maybe this attitude stems from the stories of fairy gold which turned to dust in your purse.

Financial dealing and the complexity of money systems give rise to many fine examples of Irish wit and wisdom especially when they confront the common man and woman. And nobody could be commoner that Pat, Mike and Bridget.

PAT heard that there had been a run on the bank and that his money was all gone, so he rushed to his local branch and demanded to withdraw it.

'Certainly,' said the manager, 'how would you like it?'

'Oh,' said Pat, 'if you've got it, I don't want it, but if you haven't got it, I do want it.'

BRIDGET was trying to cash a cheque in an out-of-town bank.

'Can you identify yourself, madam' asked the clerk.

'Certainly,' said Bridget, reaching into her handbag. She took out a little mirror, looked in it and declared confidently, 'Yes, it's me all right, I'd recognise me anywhere.'

MIKE was on his way home from the cattle-fair having sold all his cows.

'Did you get what you expected for them?' Pat asked.

'No,' said Mike, 'but then I didn't expect I would.'

'THE Post Office,' declared Mike, 'is the only convenient place to keep your money. You can draw it out at any instant if you give two weeks notice.'

'I CANNOT understand,' said Bridget, 'why the milk company is complaining about a shortage of glass milk bottles. I've got thousands of them at home.'

'EVERY man,' said Pat, 'should live within his income, even if he has to borrow to do so.'

MIKE went to the petrol station and asked the assistant for £10 worth of petrol. Rather ashamed of the size of his order, he remarked to the assistant, 'Before the price went up, I used to buy £20 worth.'

'LIFE insurance,' declared Pat, 'is a scheme whereby you must live poor so that you'll be rich when you die.'

'IT'S a funny thing,' said Bridget, 'that the poor, the people who need money the most, are always the very ones who never seem to have it.'

MIKE arrived home from town and announced that he had just acquired a bottle of whiskey.
'How did you manage that?' his wife asked.
'Well,' said Mike, 'it was reduced from £10 to £5 so I bought it with the £5 I saved.'

'MONEY doesn't buy happiness,' said Bridget. 'After all, a man with ten million pounds is no happier than a man with nine million pounds.'

PAT disclosed to Mike that he kept £20,000 under a mattress in his bedroom. Mike asked him why he didn't keep it in the bank, in view of all the interest he would get.
'I've thought of that,' said Pat. 'I put a little away for the interest every week too.'

PAT was returning home late one night when he was attacked by a mugger.

'Your money or your life,' shouted the mugger.

'You'd better take my life,' said Pat, 'I'm saving my money for my old age.'

BRIDGET went to the grocer's shop to buy butter.

'How much does it cost?' she asked him.

'£2 a pound,' he replied.

'In the shop down the road,' she retorted, 'it only costs £1 a pound.'

'Why don't you buy it there then?' he asked her.

'They're out of stock,' said Bridget.

'Well, when I'm out of stock,' he told her, 'I only charge 70 pence a pound.'

'All right then,' said Bridget, 'I'll come back when you're out of stock.'

BRIDGET went into the baker's shop and asked, 'Is that bread today's, because yesterday's was not?'

MIKE was offered a government grant to generate electricity by setting up a dozen windmills on his land.

He complained, 'There's hardly enough wind in this part of the country to keep a single windmill in operation, let alone a dozen of them.'

MIKE was making his will. 'I want my money divided equally between my sons and daughters,' he declared, 'and I leave the residue to my lawyer.'

PAT went into his bank and asked the manager for a loan. When the manager agreed, Pat said, 'Right that's it, I'm withdrawing all my money from this bank immediately. I can't trust an institution that is prepared to lend to such a poor risk as me.'

'A BANK,' said Bridget, 'is an institution that will lend you money only when you can produce enough collateral to prove you don't need money in the first place.'

MIKE was asked to give an estimate of how much a house he was building would cost. He included in his estimate an estimate of how much the estimate would be less than the correct figure.

PAT was drinking in a pub one night when the landlord asked him if he was going to pay for the drink he had just had.

'Did you pay for it?' asked Pat.

'Yes,' said the landlord, 'I have to pay cash for all my stock.'

'Well,' said Pat, 'there's no point in both of us paying for it, is there?'

UNDER the corrupt election system, Mike was offered £10 to vote for the first political party, £8 to vote for the second, and £5 to vote for the third. He voted for the third party because he figured they were the least corrupt.

WHEN decimal currency was introduced into Ireland, Bridget complained bitterly about the effect on people who had been used to the old system all their lives.

'Couldn't they have waited,' she asked, 'until all the old people had died?'

BRIDGET went to an auction and noticed the following entry in the catalogue:

Lot 314 One pair unique Irish silver mugs.

Lot 315 Another pair.

'DUBLIN is a great city to live in,' declared Pat, 'but it's no place for a poor man unless he has lots of money.'

'WHAT would you do if you found a million pounds, Mike?' Bridget asked.

'Well, it all depends,' said Mike, 'who had lost it. If it was a poor person, I'd certainly return it.'

MIKE was complaining that his landlord demanded one-tenth of his income as rent. 'And if he had his way,' he declared, 'he would demand as much as one-twentieth.'

BRIDGET received the following letter from her son in college:

'Dear Mother,

Send me £50 immediately.

Your loving son,

Ignatius.

P.S. I am so ashamed to have written this letter asking you for money that I sent a friend to retrieve it but the postman had already collected it. I can only hope that it was lost in the post.'

Bridget replied:

'Dear Son,

Do not worry. The letter was lost in the post.

Your loving mother,

Bridget.

P.S. I would have enclosed £50 but I have already sealed the envelope.'

— 12 —
LOVE AND MARRIAGE

IRELAND has the highest average age for marriage in the world: thirty-one for men, twenty-six for women. Courtships are long-drawn-out affairs – during which the girl decides whether or not she can do any better and the male communicates with his wife-to-be mostly verbally, hence the proliferation of wise and witty blunders . . .

YOU should have seen the engagement ring that Pat bought for Bridget. It had two diamonds, three rubies and a sapphire – all missing.

'THE only man,' said Mike, 'who knows how to manage his wife is a bachelor.'

WHEN Pat and Bridget were out courting in Pat's car one night he began to feel a bit passionate.
   'Get into the back seat,' he whispered.
   'No, Pat, I won't,' replied Bridget.
   'Why won't you get into the back seat, Bridget?' he asked.
   'Because,' said Bridget, 'I'd prefer to stay here in the front seat with you.'

'THE weaker sex,' declared Mike, 'is the stronger sex, because of the weakness of the stronger sex for the weaker sex.'

PAT and Bridget were visiting the zoo when an unmerciful fight broke out between them. Pat took to his heels and took refuge in the lion's cage.

'Come out of there, you coward,' shouted Bridget.

MIKE was delighted when his wife went on a severe diet. She was losing three pounds a week and he reckoned he would be rid of her in two years.

'I BELIEVE in chivalry,' declared Pat. 'I'll defend a woman against any man but myself.'

PAT and Bridget were having a row and although she admitted it was fundamentally her fault she said to him, 'I'm sorry, Pat, but I won't apologise.'

'HOW are you getting on with your new wife?' Mike was asked.

'Well,' he replied, 'sometimes she's better and sometimes she's worse. But from the way she carried on when she's better, I think she's better when she's worse.'

PAT was anxiously awaiting a love letter from Bridget so he went to the post office and asked the clerk if there were any letters for him.

'I'll go and see sir,' said the clerk. 'What is your name?'

'You're having me on now,' smiled Pat. 'Won't you see it on the envelope?'

WHEN Pat and Bridget were courting, Pat was very shy in popping the question and Bridget was equally slow in giving a definite answer. Finally, he wrote twice to her proposing marriage but received no reply. In desperation he wrote to her for the third time as follows:

'Dear Bridget,

This is the third time I've written to you proposing. If the answer is no, I hope you have the decency to return this letter unopened.'

'YOU think you're a beauty,' said Mike to his girlfriend one evening in exasperation, 'but I see a dozen more beautiful women than you on the street every day with my eyes shut.'

BRIDGET was so pestered by Pat's attentions when they first met that she married him just to get rid of him – and it worked beyond her wildest expectations.

MIKE and his wife were going through a stormy patch so he even initiated divorce proceedings. However, he withdrew them quickly in case his wife got to hear of it.

'WOMEN,' declared Pat, 'are mighty similar in one way – no two of them are alike.'

'MIKE is the meanest man in the world,' said a girl to Bridget.

'Why do you say that?' asked Bridget.

'Well,' said the girl, 'I've decided to refuse him if he proposes to me, and the mean old so-and-so won't propose.'

PAT died leaving his widow Bridget over £50,000. The lawyers, however, took months and months to settle the estate and Bridget was getting fed up with all the red tape and technicalities she had to wade through.

'Sometimes,' she confided in a friend, 'I'm sorry Pat ever died. Do you know I'd give £10,000 of that money just to have him back again.'

'A WIFE,' claimed Mike, 'is someone who will share with you all the troubles you wouldn't have had in the first place if you hadn't married her.'

WHEN Pat died a friend consoled Bridget by saying that at least from now on she wouldn't have to wonder where he was at night.

PAT'S LOVE LETTER TO BRIDGET
My darling Bridget,

I met you last night and you never came. Next time I'll meet you again whether you come or not. If I am there first, I'll write my name on the gatepost to let you know; and if it's you that's first rub out my name and nobody will be the wiser.

Darling Bridget, I would climb the highest mountain for your sake, and swim the widest sea. I would endure any hardship and suffer any trial to spend a moment by your side.

Your own ever loving
Pat

P.S. I'll be over to see you on Friday night if it's not raining.

AFTER an uneventful ten-year courtship Bridget said, 'Pat, don't you think it's time we were getting married?'

'Don't be a fool, woman,' said Pat, 'sure who would marry either of us at this stage of our lives?'

PAT and Bridget were having trouble with their marriage so they decided to go and see a marriage counsellor. The counsellor decided that Pat was not sufficiently aware of the female anatomy to satisfy his wife Bridget.

'For example,' the counsellor asked Pat, 'do you know where the clitoris is?'

'Is it near Mullingar?' said Pat.

'PAT,' said Bridget, 'let us go somewhere so that we can be alone together.'

'Right, Bridget,' Pat agreed, 'and afterwards we'll meet back here.'

— 13 —
CLOTHES HORSES

THE Irish have always worn clothes, even when they were naked savages without a stitch on their backs. In fact, in ancient Ireland, the clothes a man wore signified his social station. Women, too, dressed according to their marital status, and their gay and colourful outfits added a splash of interest to otherwise drab lives. Because clothes and footwear were important items in a cold climate, naturally they were talked about ...

PAT didn't hold with nudists. 'If God had meant us to be nudists,' he used to say, 'we would have been born with no clothes on.'

MIKE was looking for his hat and asked Pat to help him.

'Why it's on your head all the time,' he told him.

'Thank you,' said Mike. 'If it wasn't for you I would have gone home without it.'

BRIDGET had a blanket that was too short, so she cut several strips off the bottom and sewed them on the top.

SIGN in a shop:
'Trousers £5 a pair – they won't last long at this price.'

PAT was asked in a quiz why mohair was so expensive. He said it was because the mo was such a rare animal.

PAT was very ingenious in disguising his lack of an extensive wardrobe. For example, he always turned his socks inside out when there was a hole in the other side.

PAT and Mike were passing a nudist colony which was surrounded by a high wall, so Pat stood on Mike's shoulders to have a look inside.
'Are they men or women?' Mike asked from underneath.
'I can't tell,' said Pat, 'they haven't got any clothes on.'

BRIDGET went into a large clothing store to buy a cap for her husband Pat. Over an hour later she left the store in despair because she couldn't find one with a peak at the back.

MIKE'S shoe size is eight but he always wears nines because he finds that eights are a bit too tight for him.

'THAT fellow is so dishonest,' said Mike of a friend, 'that if he was dropped on a desert island, he would go round stealing money out of the pockets of the penniless and naked savages.'

BRIDGET bought a new £500 wool suit for Pat as a present but when she brought it home she was disgusted to find that it had a label saying '100% cotton.' She took it back to the shop and complained.

'Don't be alarmed, madam,' said the man in the shop, 'it's merely a device to fool the moths.'

MIKE claimed he had a belt with only one end because he had cut the other end off.

BRIDGET announced to the family that she had just bought a new pair of waterproof gloves. 'Now,' she boasted, 'I can wash my hands without getting them wet.'

BRIDGET was having great difficulty with the buttons on her new dress. She complained that she never had a dress that buttoned behind before.

PAT was shopping in the city and saw a £1,000 toupé of luxuriant hair in a shop window.

'Isn't it amazing,' he said to Bridget, 'how they can make hair grow on that thing but not on your head.'

— 14 —
PAPAL BULLS
AND HOLY COWS

RELIGION *has always been a strong feature of Irish life but the earthly limitations of language are exposed when we begin to discuss divine subjects, eternal and infernal . . .*

PAT decided to become an atheist and one day he was heard to remark, 'I wonder if God knows I'm an atheist? I wish to God I could believe in God.'

MIKE was telling a joke about a man who received a letter which said, 'If you can't read this note, take it to the parish priest and he will read it for you.'
   'I get it,' laughed Bridget. 'What if the parish priest was out when he arrived with the letter?'

BRIDGET was explaining the Christmas story to one of her children. Showing him a picture in an illustrated bible, she said, 'And this is where the baby Jesus was born on the first Christmas Eve.'

THE following advertisement is said to have appeared in a Northern Irish newspaper:- 'Man and woman wanted to milk two cows, both Protestant.'

MIKE was leading the evening prayers in his household. He intoned, 'Let us now pray for people in uninhabited areas of the world.'

'DID you go to see the Pope when he visited Ireland?' Bridget asked a friend.

'No,' said the friend.

'What a pity,' said Bridget, 'if only you had been there to see how wonderful it was, you would have been sorry to have missed it.'

THE first time that Bridget met a married Protestant clergyman with a family she was scandalised.

'Calls himself father,' she said indignantly, 'and him with four children.'

'TELL me,' said Pat to the bishop, 'is God all-powerful?'

'He is that, Pat,' said the bishop, sipping his pint.

'Well, tell me,' said Pat, 'could he make a stone so heavy he couldn't lift it?'

'He could,' said the bishop, 'and then, just to prove he was all-powerful, he would go and lift it.'

ONE of the best 'papal bulls' on record concerns the Vatican's Index of Forbidden Books. The Index proved such popular reading with those seeking improper reading material, that in the next edition the Index itself was included in the Index!

MIKE was on his deathbed so he told his wife to send for the Minister because he wanted to become a Protestant.

'Why Mike,' asked his wife, 'when you have been a

staunch Catholic all your life?'

'I'd much prefer,' groaned Mike, 'to see one of them so-and-so's going rather than one of us.'

'ISN'T one man as good as another?' the priest said to Pat.

'He is, father,' agreed Pat, 'and a great deal better.'

BRIDGET was upset by the way people rushed for the doors of the church the very moment proceedings were finished.

'There would be no problem,' she said, 'if they all sat quietly in their places like me until the crush had gone.'

A BELFAST widow was describing her Orange husband's last few minutes on earth. 'First of all,' she wept, 'he asked for his wee sash, and then he asked for his wee fife. Then he asked for his wee drum, and shouting "To hell with the pope," he flew straight into the arms of Jesus.'

'EVERY man,' declared Pat, 'should have freedom of conscience and behaviour, and those that don't want to should be forced to.'

BRIDGET was consoling a neighbour whose husband had died.

'I'm sorry to hear that your husband is gone to heaven,' she told her, 'and that his friends and relatives will never see him again.'

MIKE'S son went to England and got a job in a crematorium. He wrote home to say that he was having the time of his life – burning Protestants and getting paid for it.

PAT was continually complaining despite the fact that he was in a state of perfect health.

'You ungrateful fellow,' said his more religious wife Bridget, 'get on your knees and thank God you are still on your feet.'

MIKE was fed up with all the morbid sermons about death that he kept hearing in Church.

'Death,' he declared, 'is something we can all live without.'

IRISH bulls have penetrated right into the Bible itself. In the Book of Isaiah, chapter 37, verse 36, we read: 'Then the angel of the Lord went forth, and smote in the camp of the Assyrians a hundred and four score and five thousand: and when they arose early in the morning, behold, they were all dead corpses.'

In the New Testament we read: 'And he said "saddle me an ass," so they saddled him.'

PAT'S five-year-old little boy, who was a Catholic, was staying with some Protestant friends. One evening the woman of the house gave him a bath which he shared with a little four-year-old girl. When he returned home he said to his father, 'I never knew there was such a difference between Catholics and Protestants.'

— 15 —
WORK

WORK *is a four-letter word in Ireland and the average Irishman likes work so much he can sit down all day watching someone else doing it. There is all the difference in the world between an Irishman looking for a job and looking for work. Traditionally, the Irish in England and the United States have been connected with the building and construction industries and it is from this source that most of the wit and wisdom in this chapter arise.*

PAT applied for a job at the building site and was being interviewed by the foreman. 'It's like this,' he told him. 'I can't give you a start today, but if you come back tomorrow I might have something for you. The position is that I have a fellow here today who hasn't turned up for work. If he doesn't come again tomorrow, I'll send him home, and you can have his job.'

MIKE got a job on a building site and one of the first things he saw was the following notice:
HOLES PAINTED WHITE ARE NOT TO BE DRILLED

BRIDGET read the following household hint in a magazine. 'Grease stains on clothes may be removed with ammonia, but old stains, being hard to remove, must be treated as soon as they are made.'

PAT and Mike were building a house together but Pat kept throwing away all the nails.

'Why are you doing that?' Mike asked him.

'These nails are defective,' said Pat, 'the heads are on the wrong end.'

'You fool,' said Mike, 'those are for the other side of the house.'

BRIDGET was a do-it-yourself enthusiast, so she bought a household ladder that was advertised as follows: 'This ladder will last forever if you don't wear out the rungs with use.'

'THEY'RE not building houses like they used to,' maintained Pat. 'Show me any modern building that has lasted as long as the old ones.'

MIKE had an axe that he had inherited from his great grandfather and it had been in continuous use in his family for over a hundred years. In that time it had only five new heads and six new handles.

PAT had built a barn for his donkey but found that the donkey refused to go in because its ears were catching on the top of the doorway. When Bridget suggested that he should dig a little trench along the doorway Pat retorted, 'Don't be stupid, woman, it's the donkey's ears that are causing the problem, not his feet.'

PAT and Mike were working on a building site and Pat was heard to call out to his workmate, 'Don't come down that ladder, Mike, I've taken it away.'

BRIDGET'S doorbell was broken so she sent for an electrician. A week later she rang him to ask why he hadn't called.

'I called three times,' he told her, 'but nobody answered the bell.'

PAT and Mike were way behind schedule on a building job so they decided to increase their work rate.

'We'll finish this house this morning,' declared Pat, 'even if it takes us all day to do so.'

PAT applied for a job on a building site and told the foreman he had forty years experience.

'How old are you?' asked the foreman.

'Thirty-five,' replied Pat.

'How do you explain that then?' asked the foreman.

'I did a lot of overtime,' said Pat.

PAT got a job on a building site but he got the sack because he left without giving notice.

BRIDGET was rushing round her kitchen with a paint brush sloshing paint all over the walls. She was trying to finish the job before all the paint ran out.

PAT and Mike joined the local fire brigade and one night they were called to quell a big fire. As they poured water on the flames, Pat said, 'Take it easy a bit, Mike, and let it burn up so we can see what we are doing.'

MIKE lived all his life in a lighthouse and every hour on the hour the bell rang. One night he went to sleep at midnight and at 1 a.m. the bell failed to ring. Mike sat bolt upright in his bed and said, 'What was that?'

PAT and Mike were painting a house and Mike was working on a high ladder painting an upstairs window.

'Have you a good grip on that paintbrush, Mike?' asked Pat.

'I have indeed, Pat,' replied Mike.

'Then hold on tight,' said Pat, 'because I'm taking the ladder away.'

THE great lexicographer Samuel Johnson must have lived in an Irish building because in his famous dictionary he defined the attic as the highest room in the house, and the garret as the room above the attic.

BRIDGET returned home to find that some joker had sealed up the keyhole of her front door and painted it over.

'Whoever stole my keyhole,' she commented, 'it won't do him much good, because I've got the key in my pocket.'

MIKE had been killed on the building site when a steam-hammer fell from a great height and hit him on the chest.

'I'm not surprised,' said Bridget, 'Mike always had a weak chest.'

BRIDGET was attending a lecture on archaeology at her local college. 'Look at the great cities of antiquity,' thundered the lecturer. 'Some of them have vanished so utterly that it is doubtful whether they have ever existed at all.'

PAT was working on a building site and the foreman asked him to dispose of some rubble, so Pat dug a hole.

'Now where are you going to put the dirt from the hole?' asked the foreman.

'I'll dig another hole,' said Pat.

'How will that help?' asked the foreman again.

'I'll dig the other hole deeper,' said Pat.

— 16 —

THE TALE END
OF THE BULL

DURING a long hot summer there was a sudden rainstorm. Pat remarked, 'An hour of this rain will do as much good in ten minutes as a month of it would do in a fortnight at any other time of the year.'

MIKE was at a concert given by the world famous blind pianist. 'It wouldn't matter if he wasn't blind,' said Mike, 'because I watched him all the time and he never looked at the piano once.'

MIKE'S lad Sean was asked to write an essay about his favourite bird. He chose the cuckoo and began as follows, 'The cuckoo is an unusual bird. He doesn't lay his own eggs and he lives in a clock.'

BRIDGET is not superstitious – she's afraid it might bring her bad luck.

PAT was explaining to Bridget the difficulties of making contact with the inhabitants of the planets and stars.

'We will never be able to communicate with the beings of outer space,' he told her, 'until we can first notify them with a signal to be on the lookout for a communication.'

MIKE was speaking on a political platform in a large hall.

'Can all you people at the back of the hall hear me?' he shouted.

'No, we can't,' they shouted back.

MIKE was in the big city without a watch so he asked a passing man for the time.

'It's half past two,' replied the man.

'That's funny,' said Mike, 'I've been asking people that all day, and getting different answers, and to prove it, I've written them all down on this piece of paper.'

NEWSPAPER report: 'Because of bad weather the sun was not visible in Ireland during its recent total eclipse.'

ACCORDING to the Dubliners, the Irish Navy is the only navy on earth where all the sailors go home for their tea.

NOTICE in a newspaper: 'Because of lack of space, several births have been postponed until next week.'

PAT received a new tool-kit and on comparing it with the invoice found that it contained everything except a chisel which was missing, so he took it back to the shop.

'I have it here,' said the shopkeeper. 'I just took it out to open the case with it.'

MIKE was looking at a photograph of his ancestral home.

'That is the house,' he said proudly, 'that my father built and my grandfather was born in.'

MIKE was the caretaker of a building that was on fire.

'Let me in, let me in,' said a brash young reporter, 'I represent the press and I've come to report on the fire.'

'Go home,' said Mike. 'You can read all about it in the papers in the morning.'

PAT was talking about his visit to the Vatican. He told his listeners that it is a Mecca for tourists.

MIKE got his rates bill from the County Council and it had a £25 charge for sewage, so he stormed round to the Council and told them that he hadn't received any sewage from them.

'We called to deliver it but you were not in,' said the official.

'Couldn't you have put it through the letterbox?' said Mike.

BRIDGET was reading *The Cork Examiner*. 'Isn't it amazing,' she said to Pat, 'how just enough things seem to happen every day to fill the newspaper.'

MIKE heard that by putting a brick in your toilet cistern you could conserve water. So he put a brick in his petrol tank.

PAT was out walking one day when he saw a sign
REFUSE TO BE PUT IN THIS LITTER BIN.

Pat got into the bin saying, 'Nobody tells me what to do in my own country.'